this book belongs to:

ANIMALS

ANT

BEAR

COW

DOLPHIN

ELEPHANT

FROG

GIRAF

HORSE

Jellyfish

LION

MONKEY

OWL

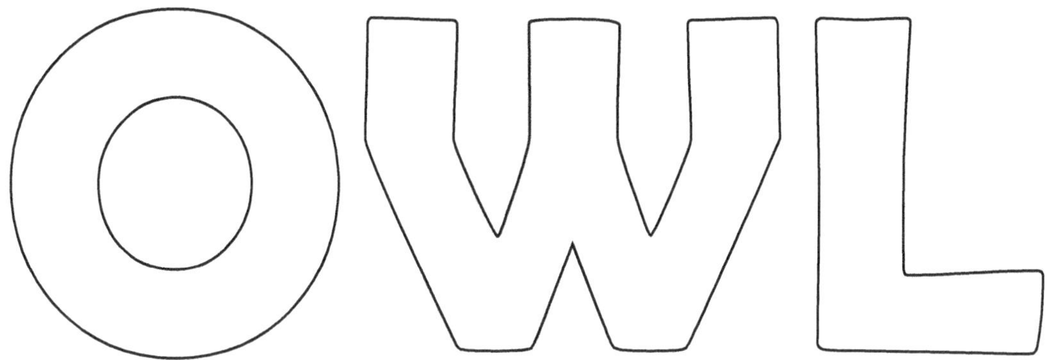

OWL

Rhinoceros

SEAL

TURTUL

WOLF

ZEBRA

NUMBERS

123

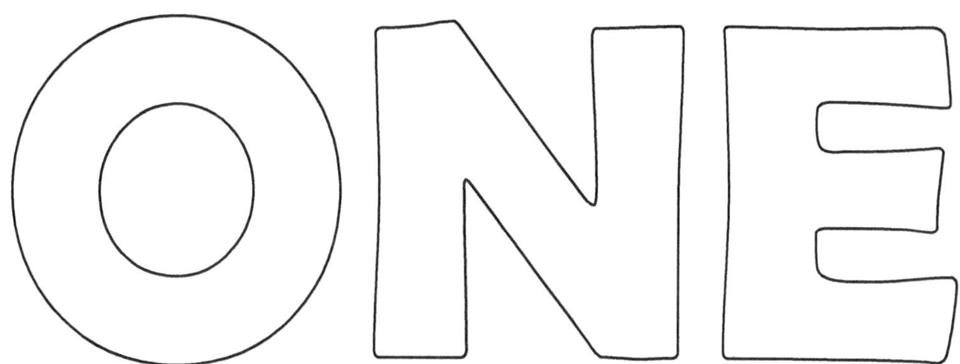
ONE

1

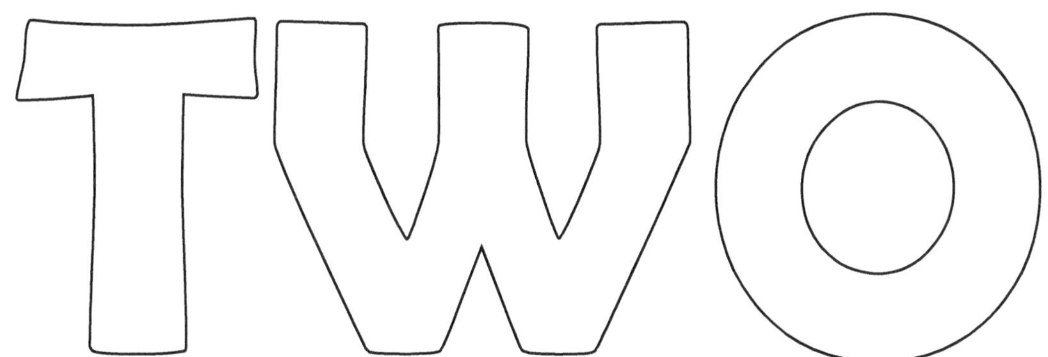

THREE

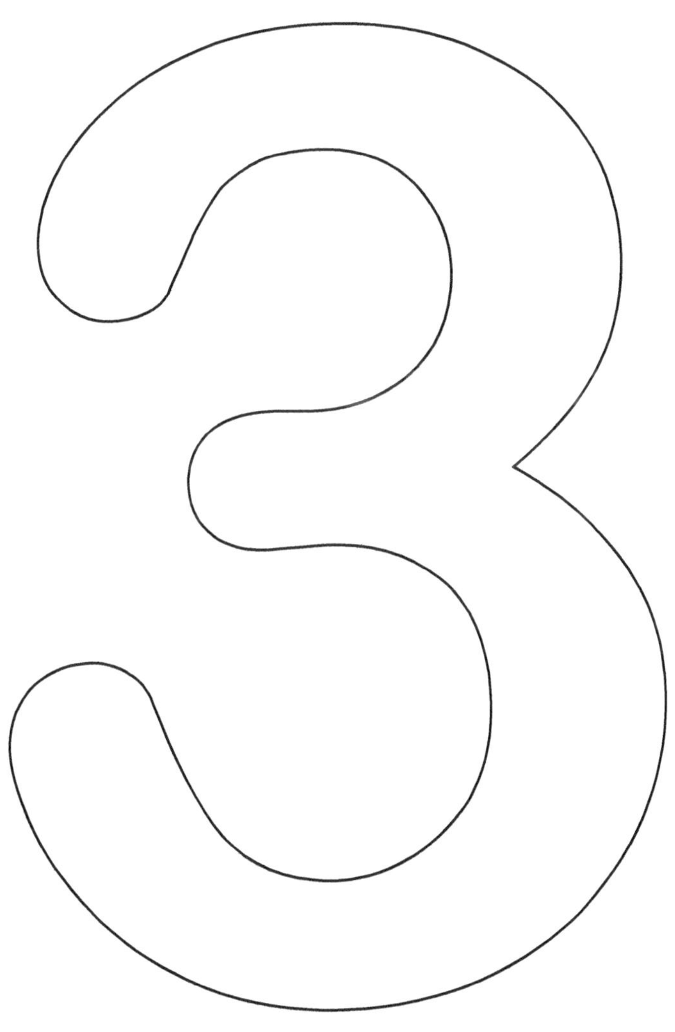

FOUR

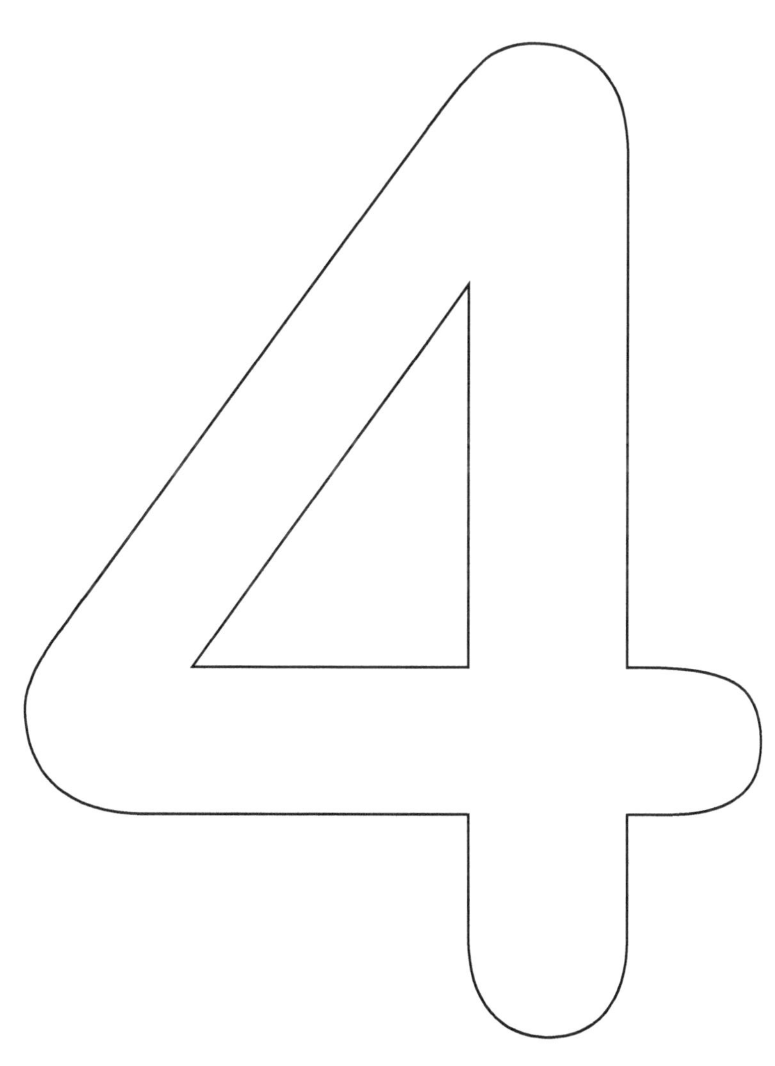

FIVE

SIX

SEVEN

EIGHT

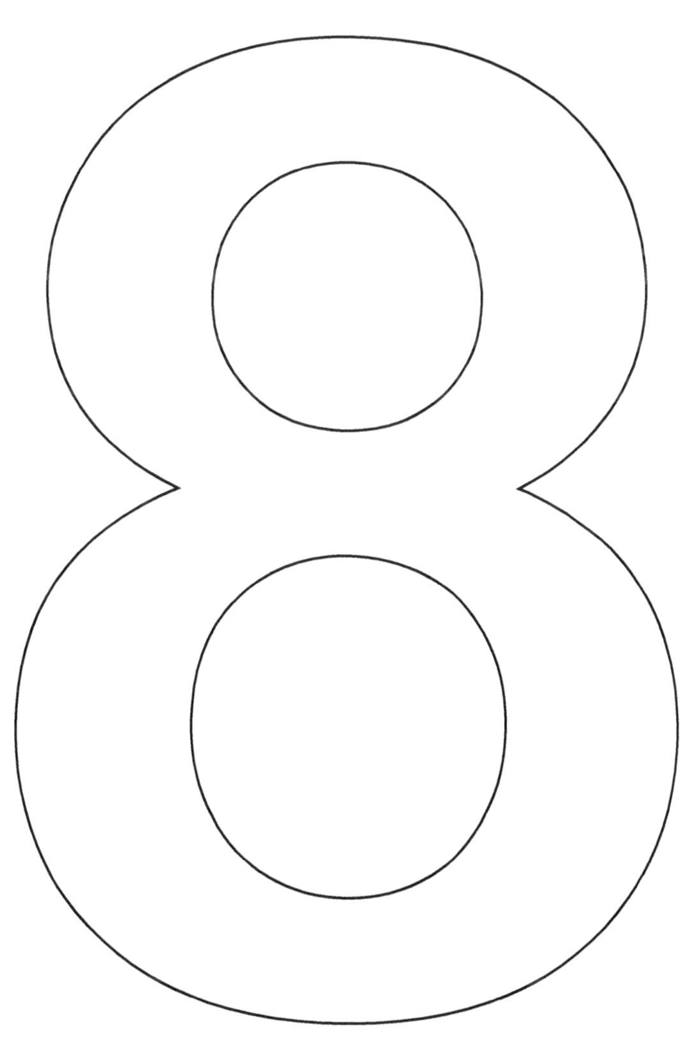

NINE

TEN

ELEVEN

11

TWELVE

FIFTEEN

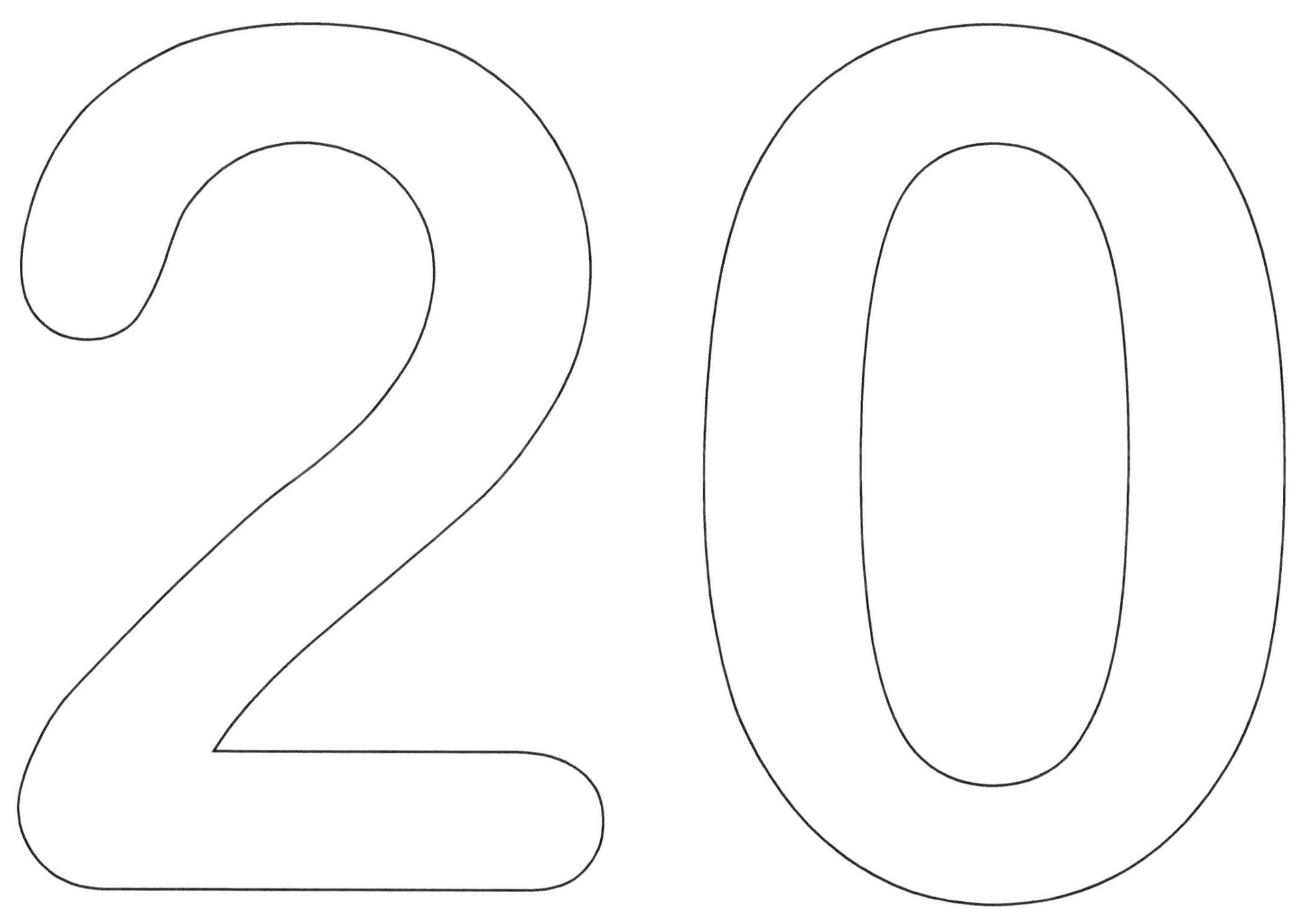
TWENTY
20

TWENTY ONE

THIRTY

30

THIRTY ONE

FORTY

40

FORTY ONE

FIFTY

50

FIFTY ONE

51

SEXTY

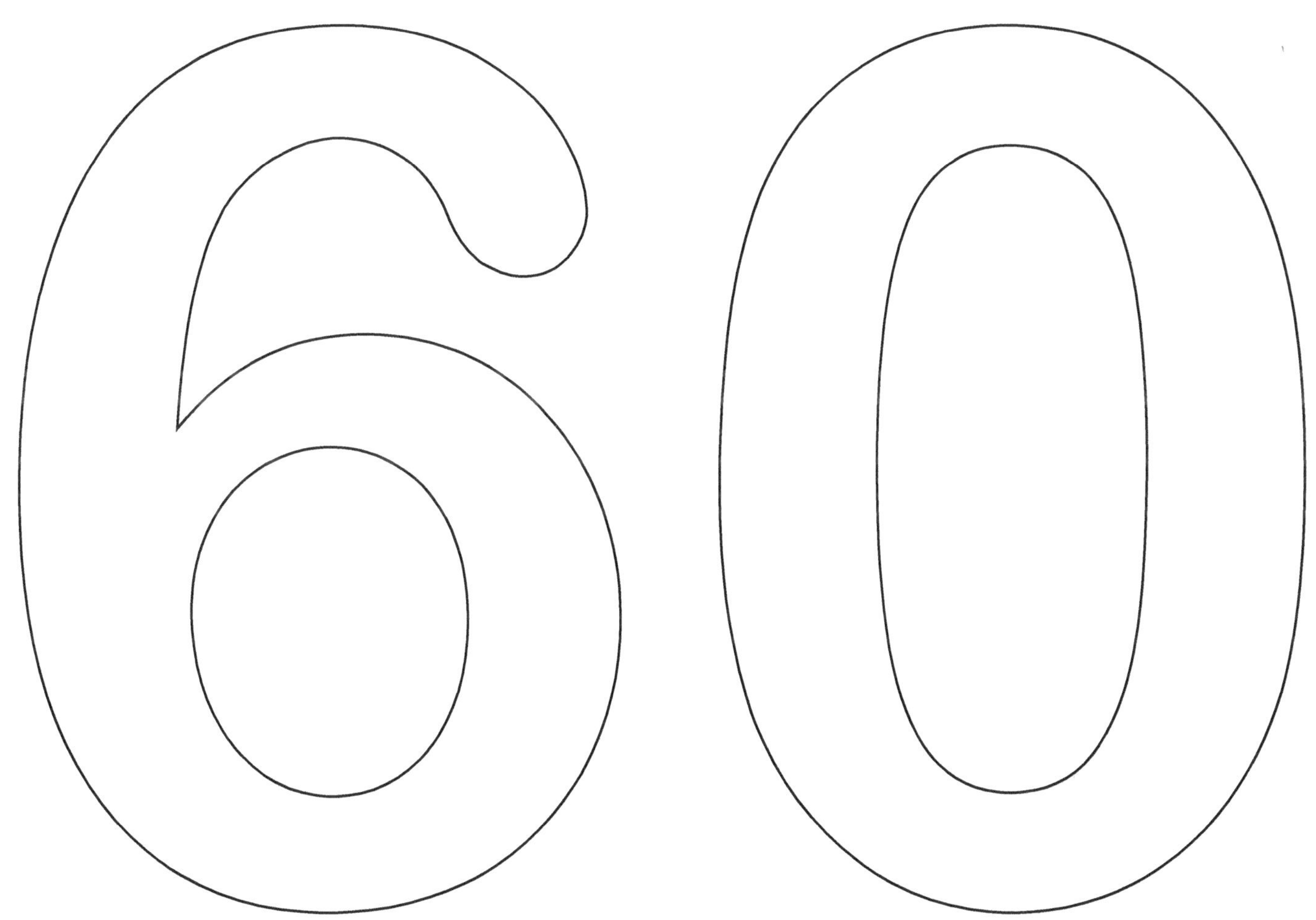

SEXTY ONE

SEVENTY
70

SENTY ONE

EIGHTY

EIGHTY ONE

NINETY

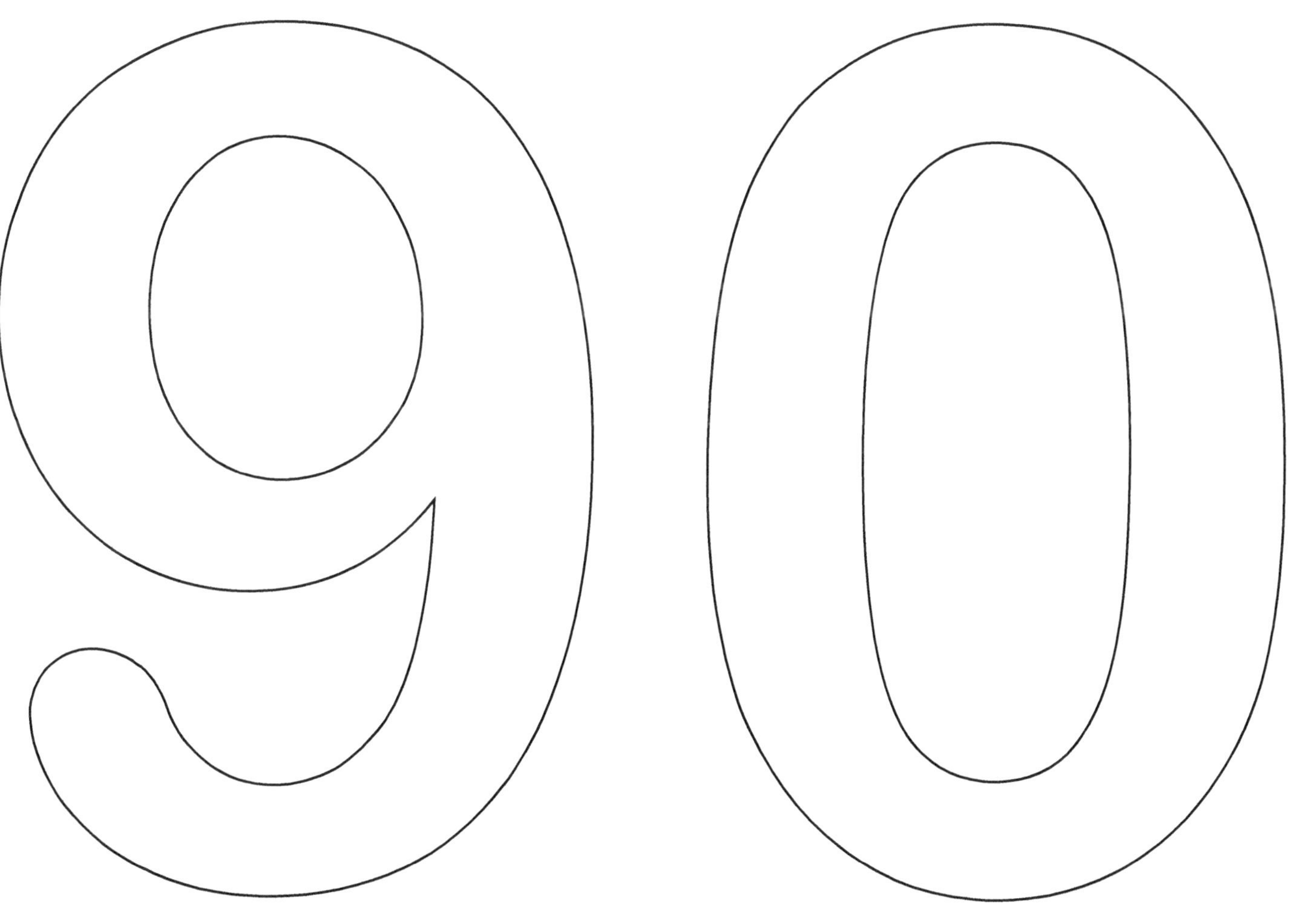

NINETY ONE

ONE HUNDRED

FRUITS

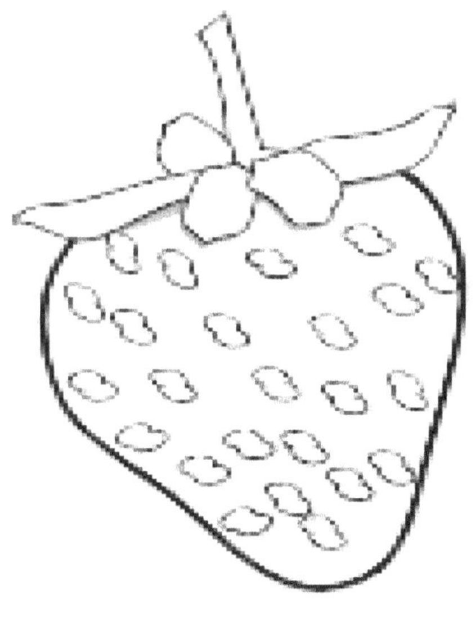

LEMON

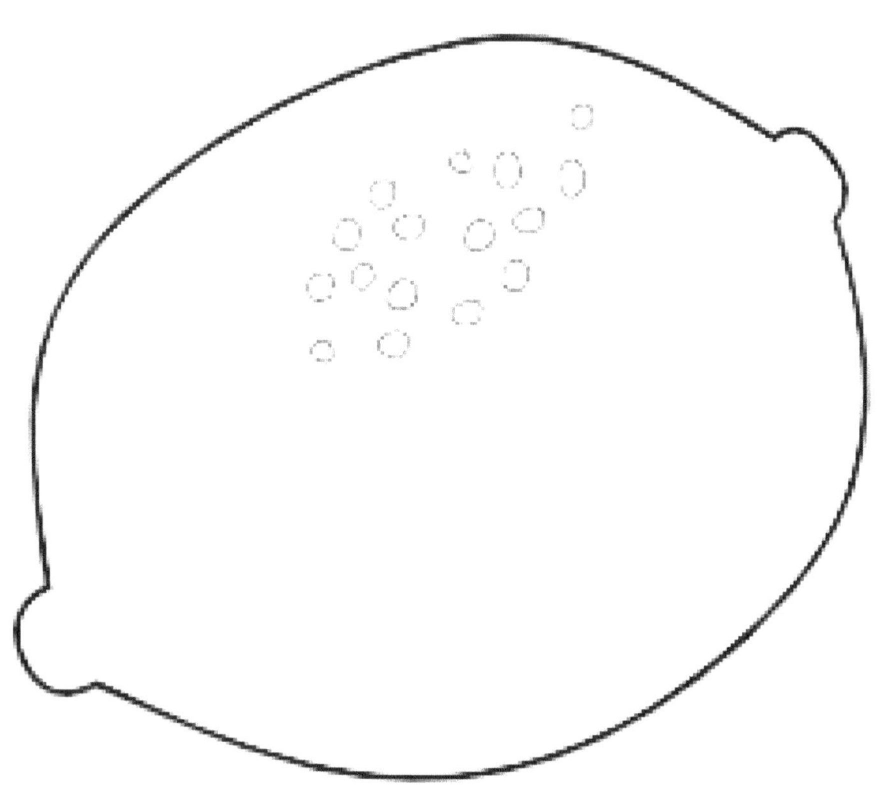

GRAPE

PLUMS

BANANA

STRAWBERRY

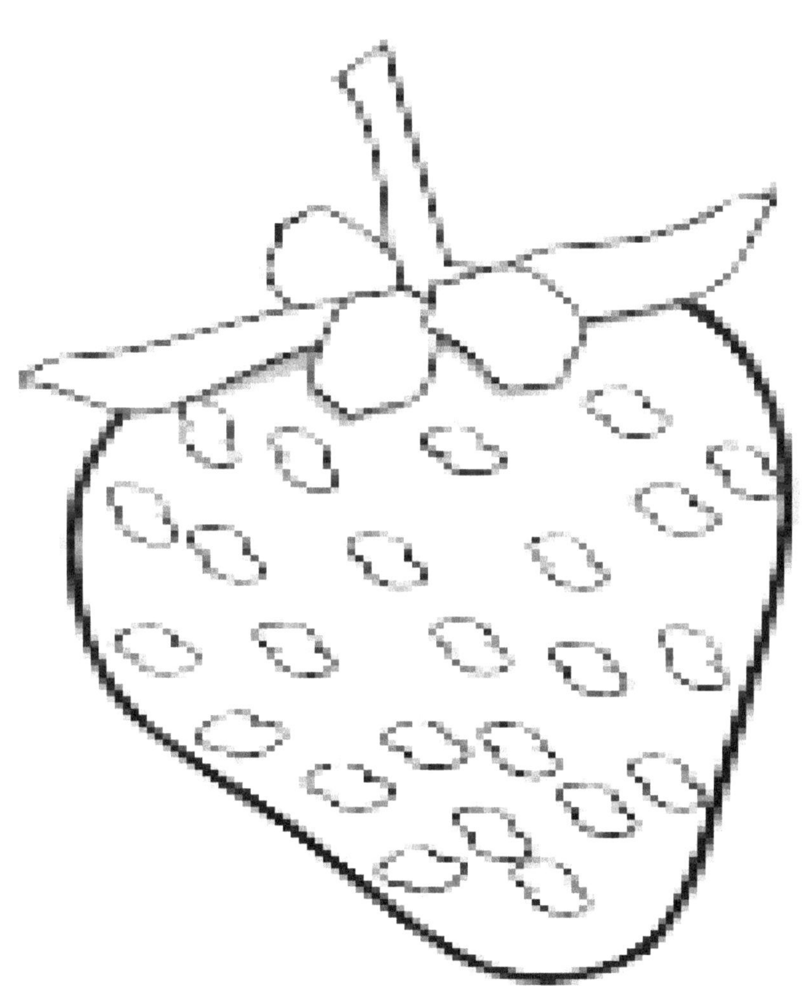

ORANGE

APPLE

PEACH

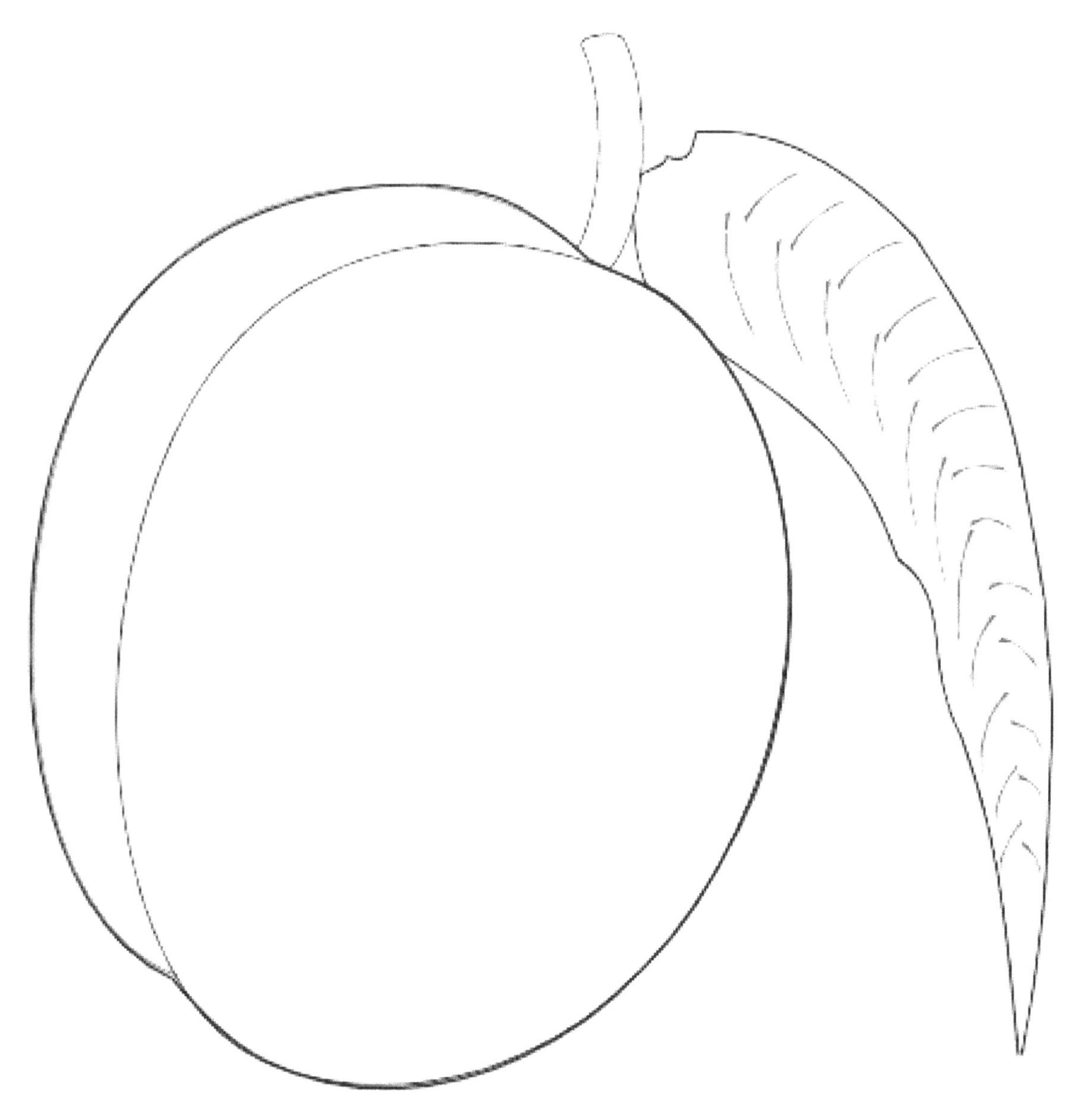

WATERMELON

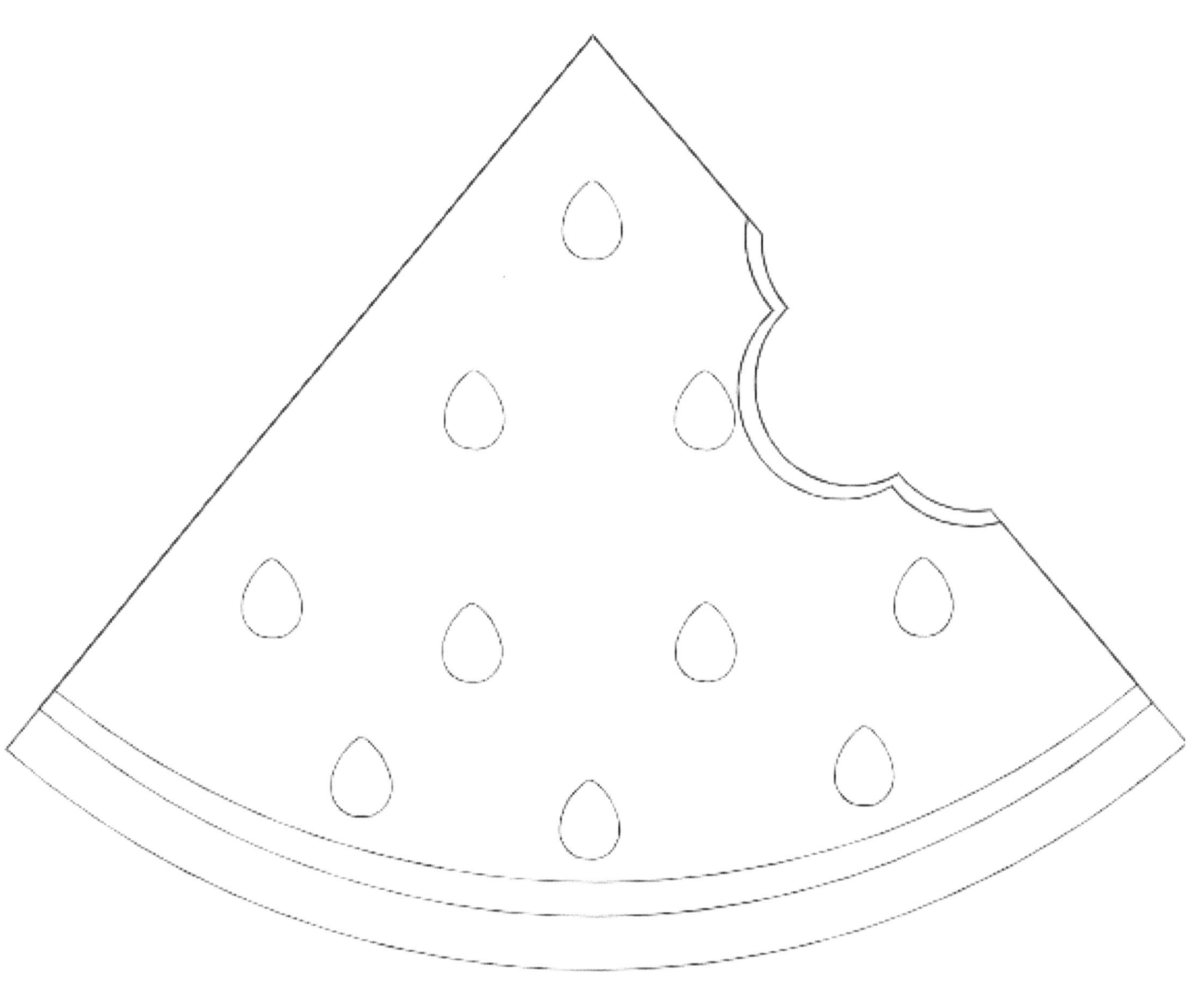

AVOCADO

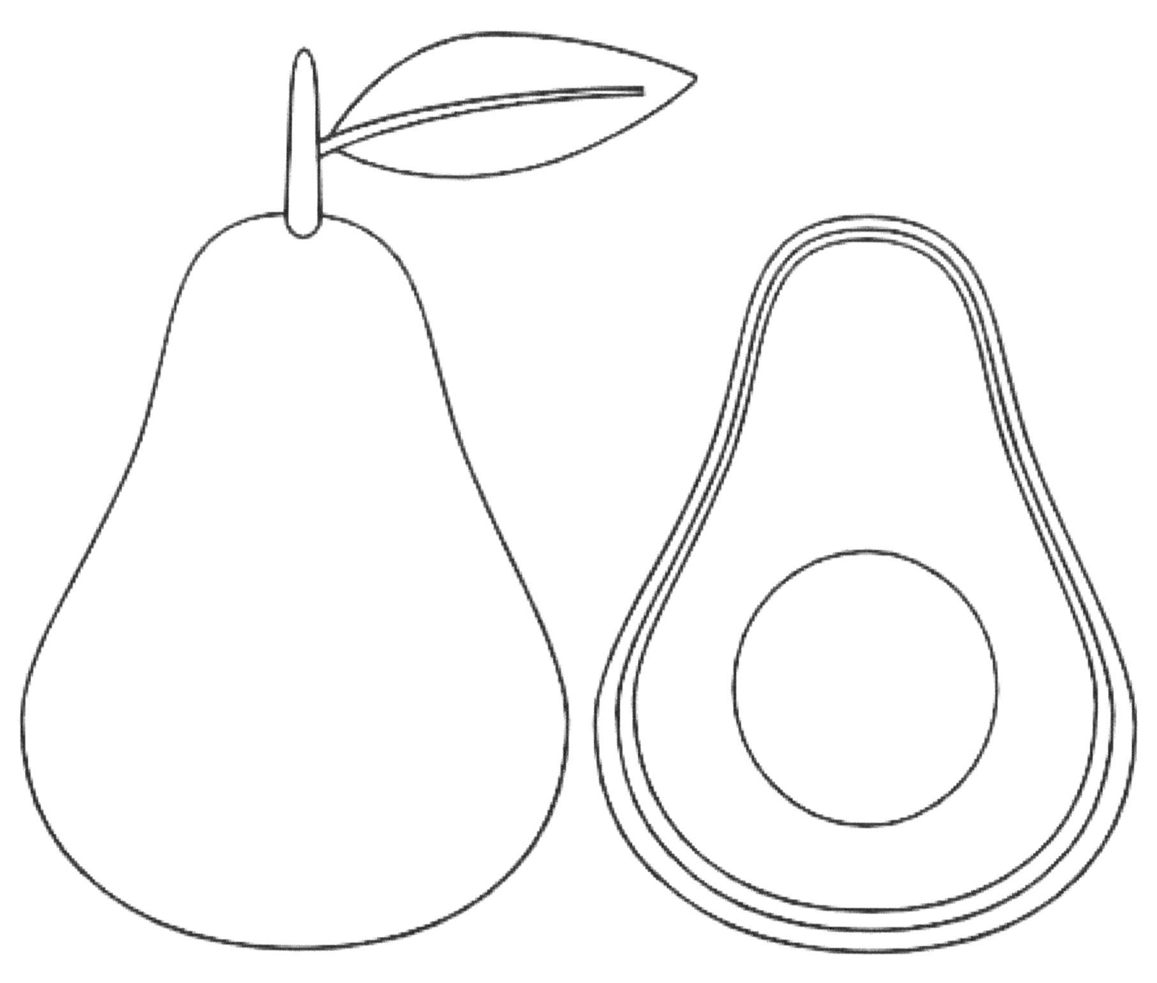

CHERRY

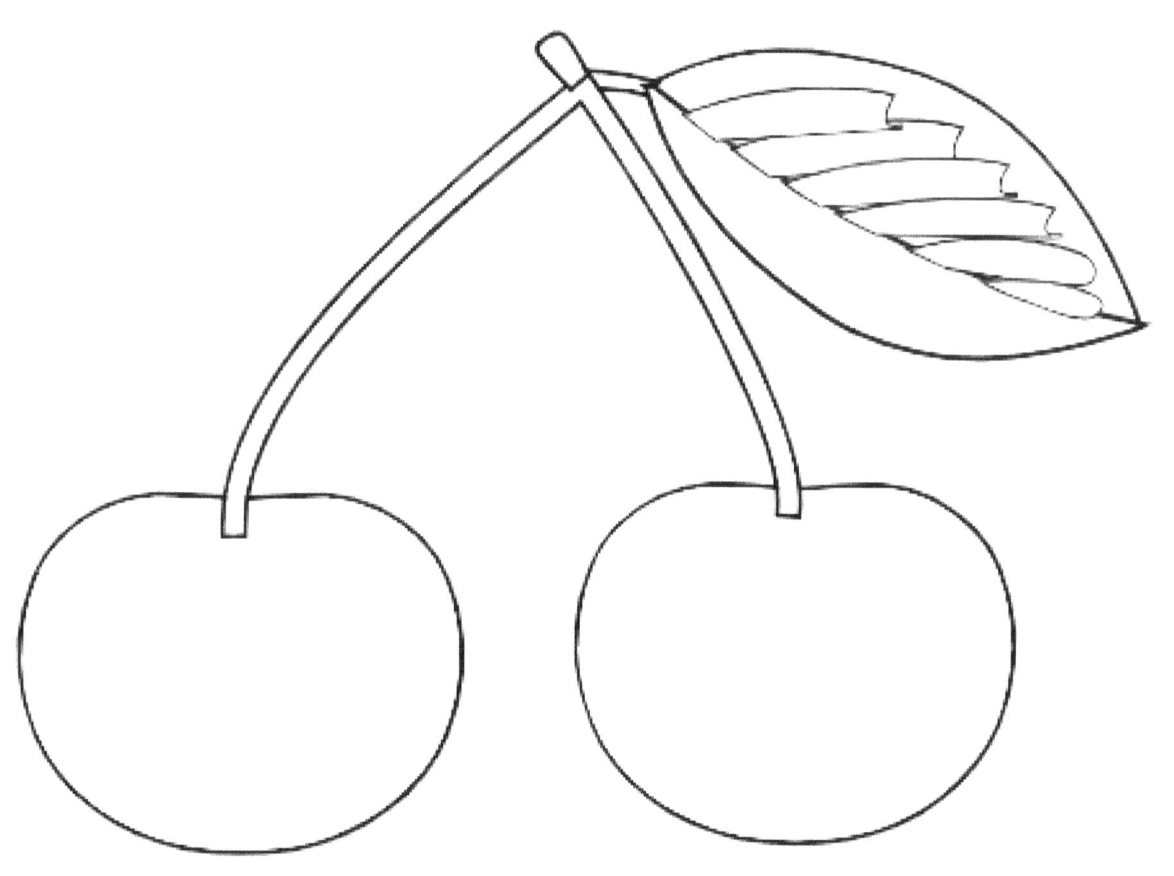

VEGETABLES

AUBERGINE

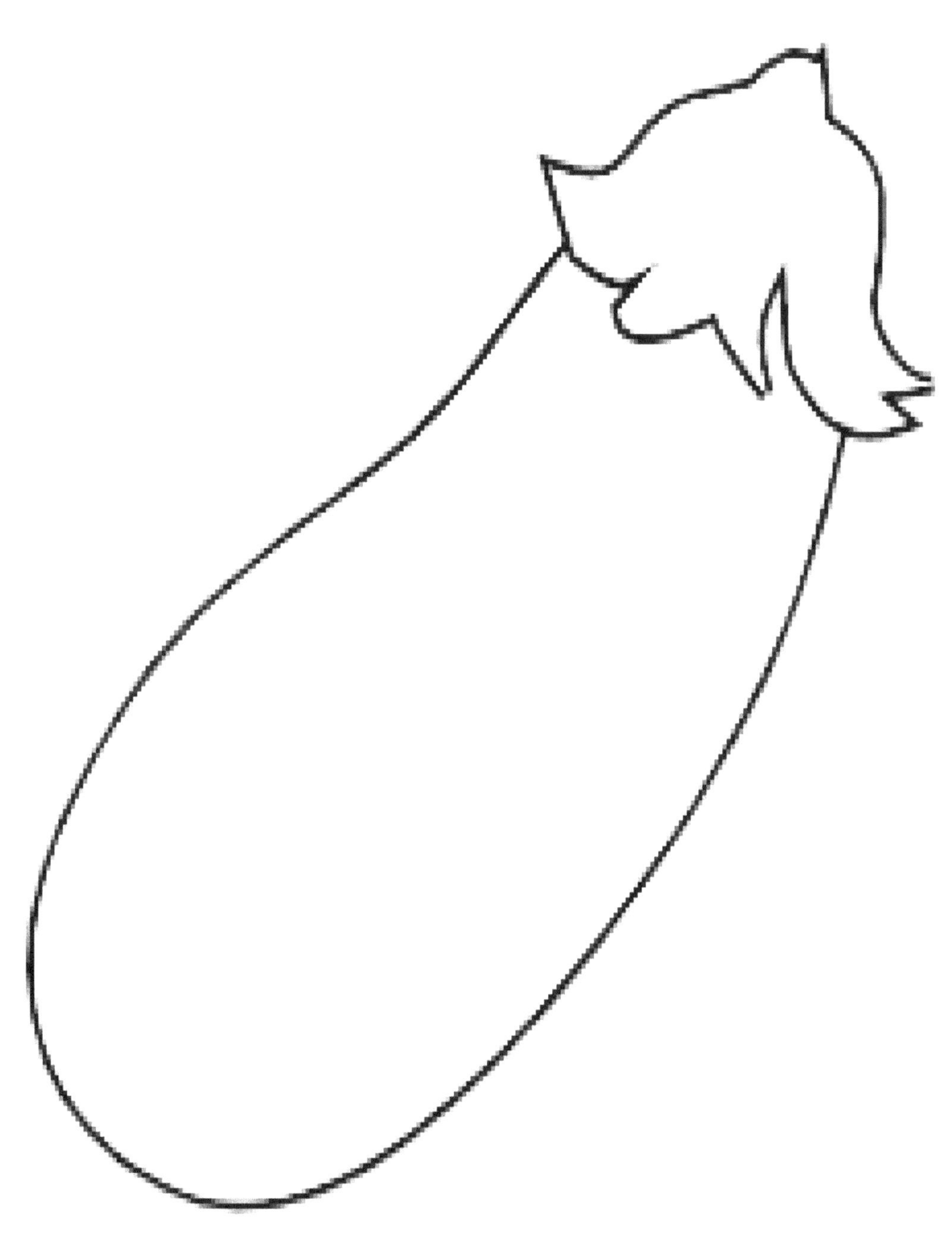

CUCUMBER

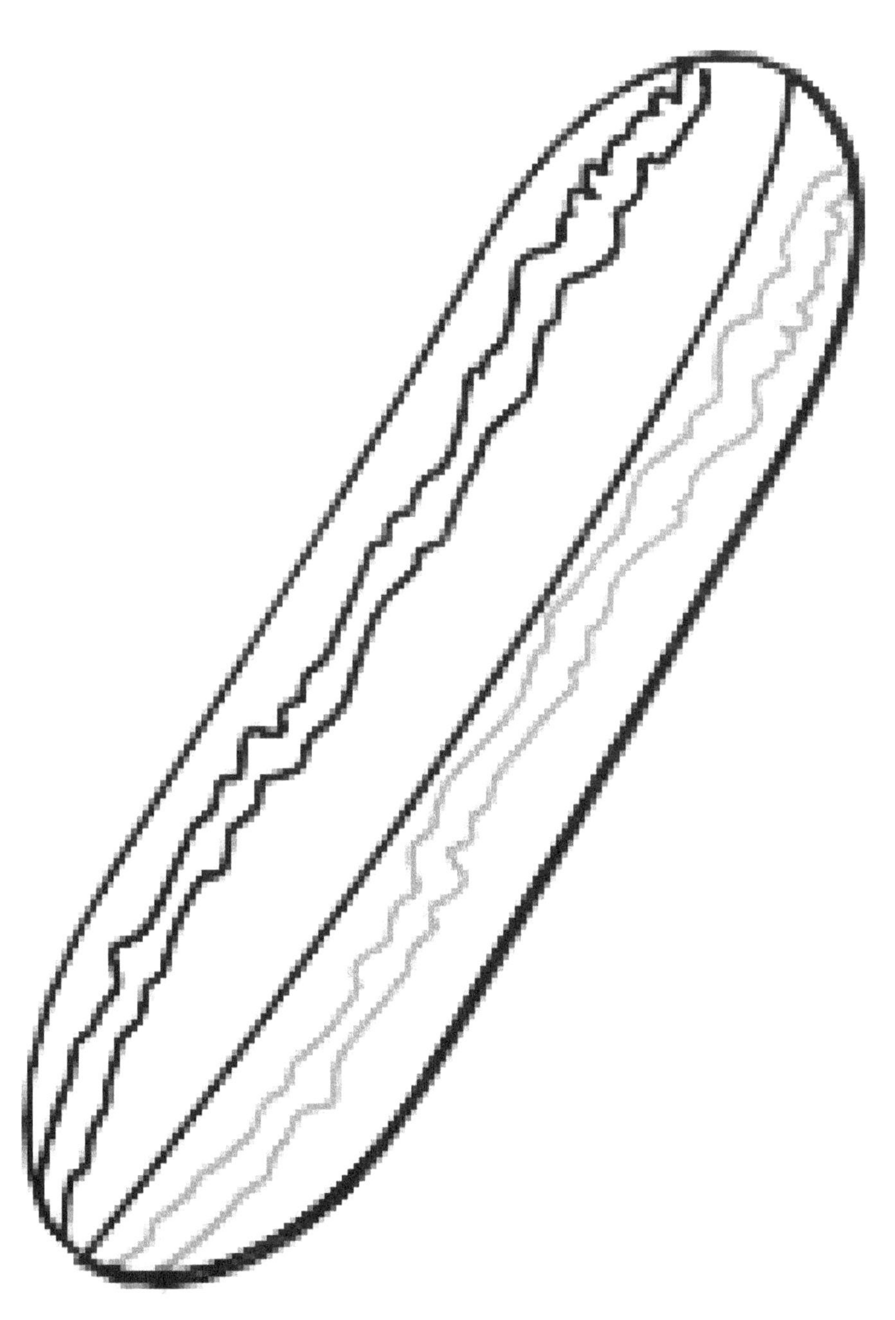

PEPPER

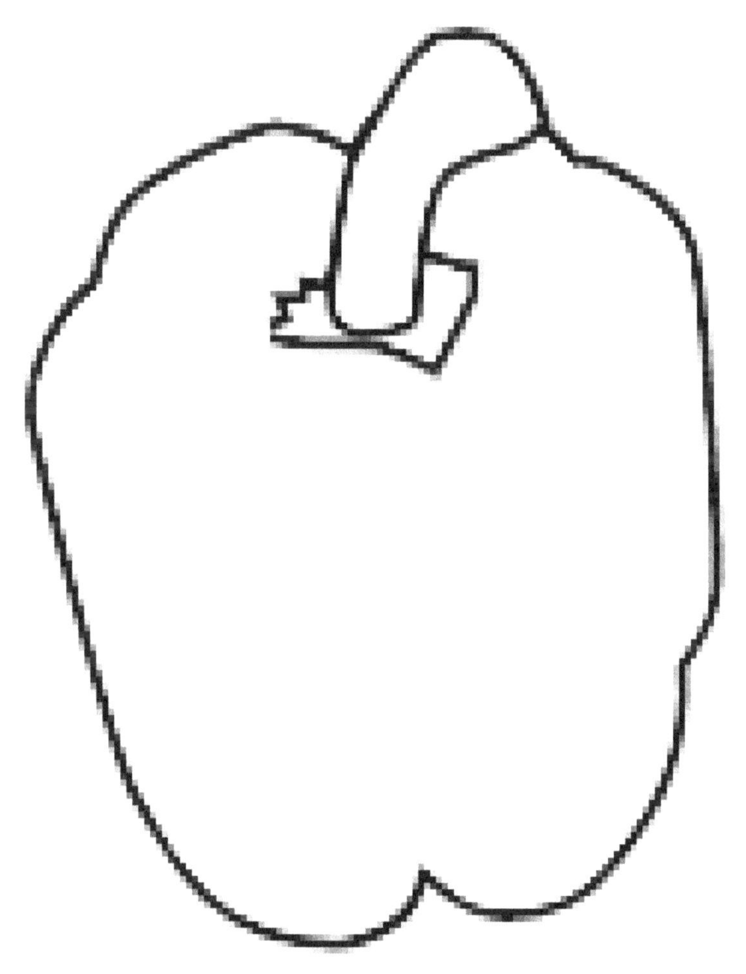

TOMATO

CARROT

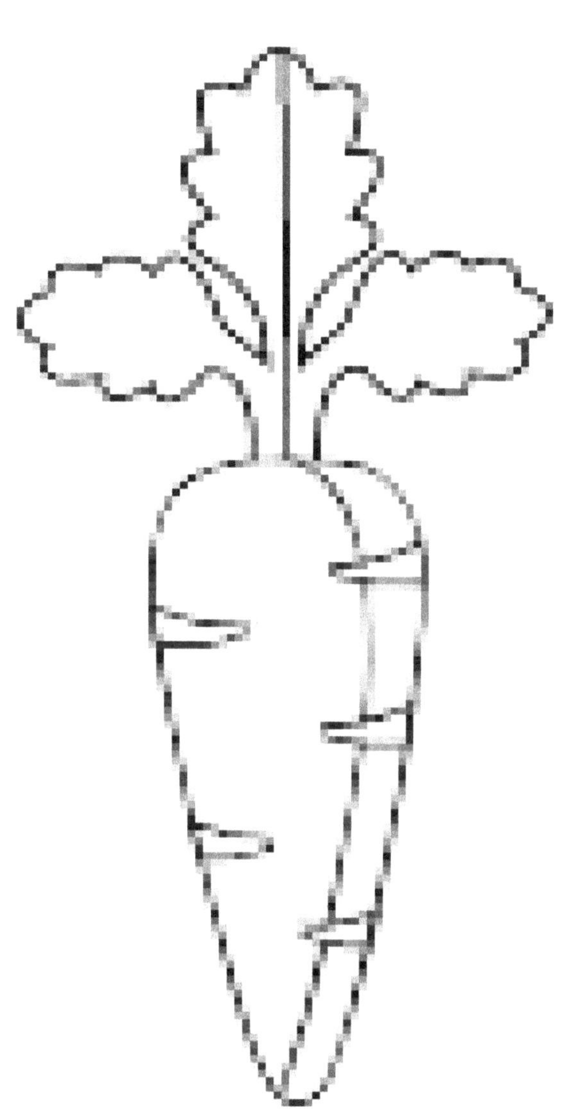

BEETROOT

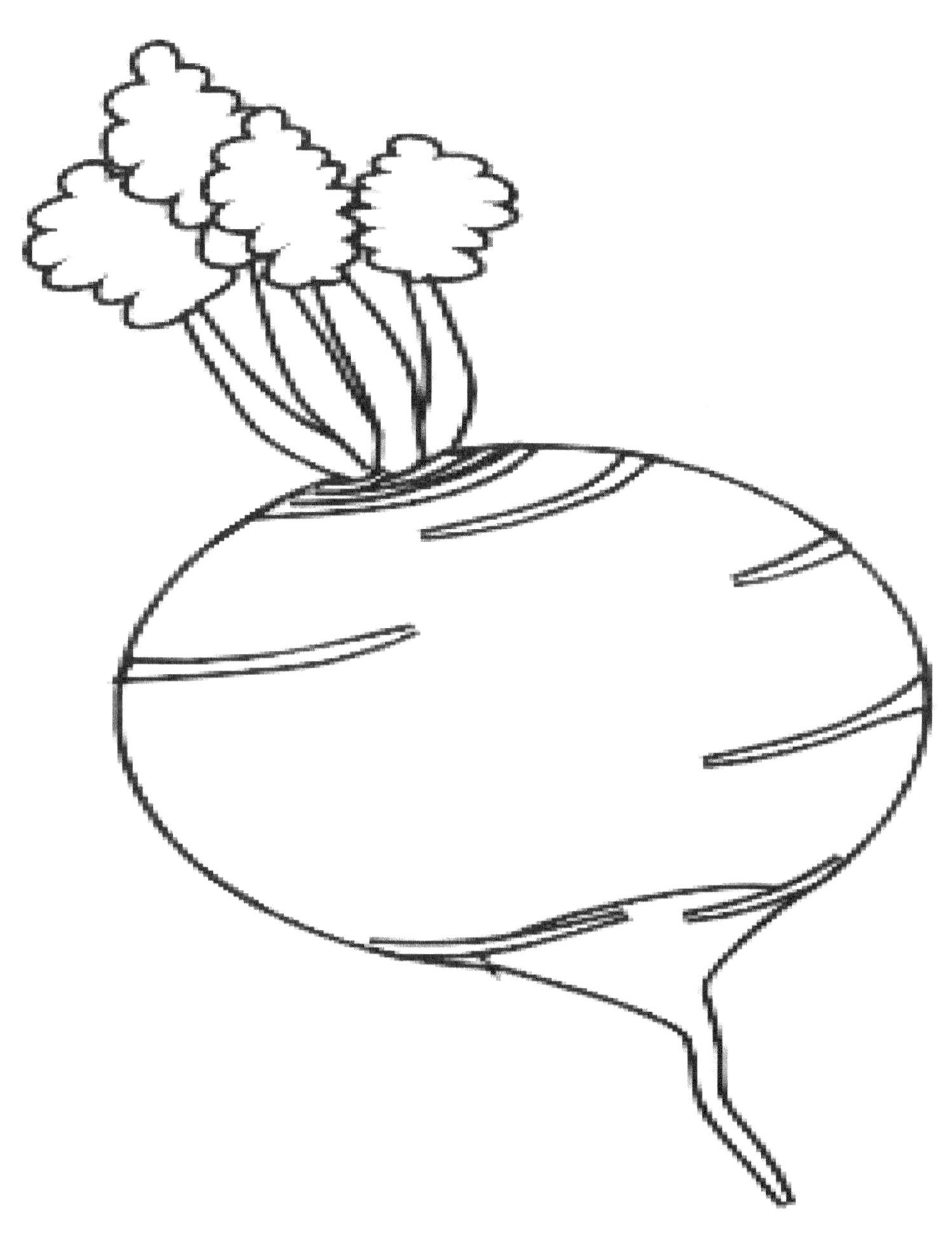

PUMPKIN

ONION

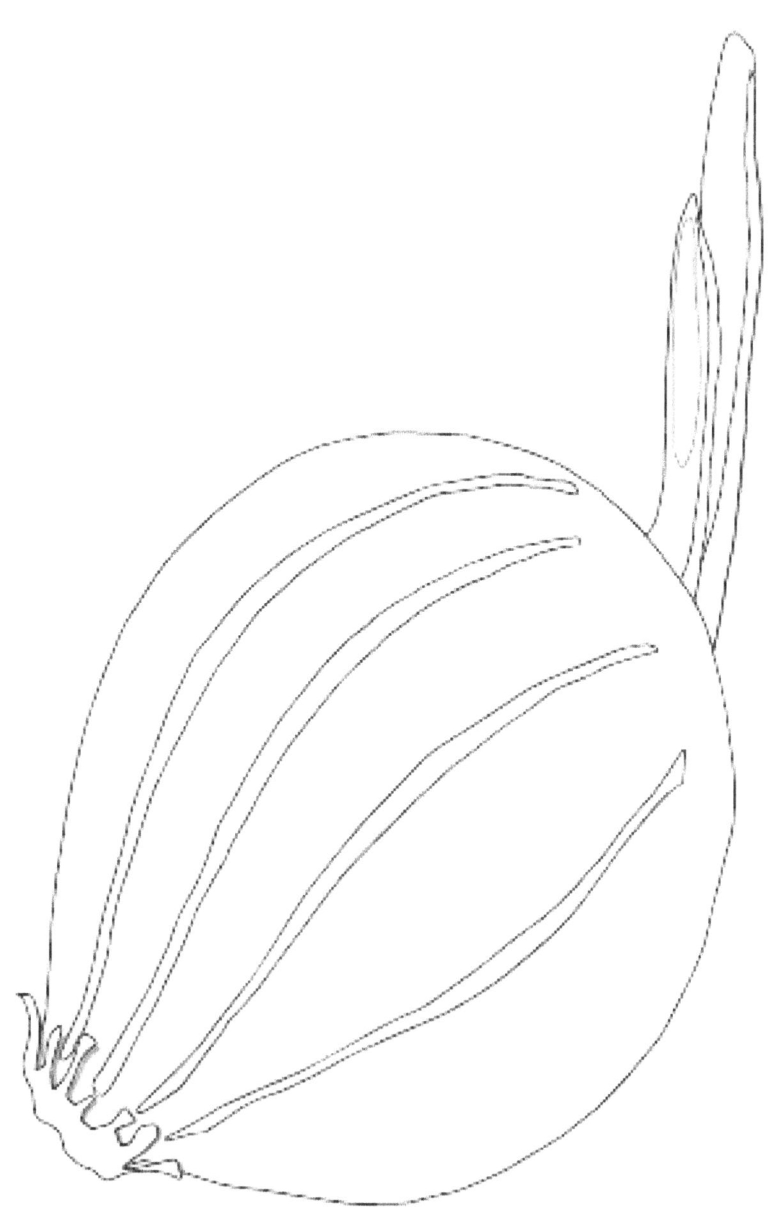

POTATO

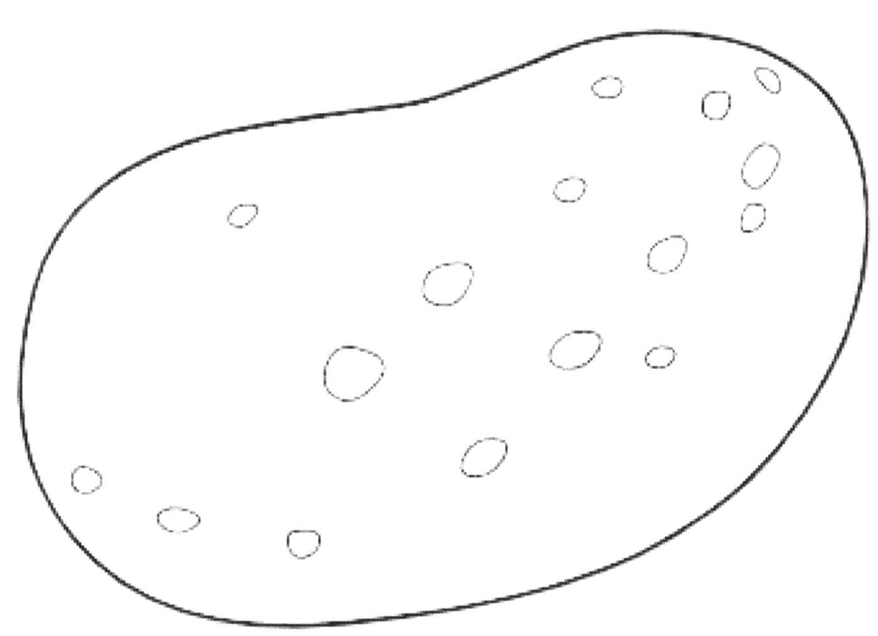